# STRONG VOICE

## STRONG VOICE

A Quick reference to improve your writing and impress readers

### Ann Everett

Copyright 2014 by Ann Everett All rights reserved

First print edition, June 2014

ISBN-13:978-1499719291

ISBN-10:1499719299

No part of this publication may be reproduced or distributed in print or electronic form without prior permission of the author. Please respect the hard work of the author and do not participate in or encourage the piracy of copyrighted materials.

Book cover design by: Reagan E. Ball 2014
Stock purchased by Ann Everett from Dollarphotoclub.com

# ABOUT THE AUTHOR

Ann Everett writes mysteries, new adult romance, and romantic comedy with a dose of Texas twang and Southern sass. She lives in Northeast Texas, where she drinks too many Diet Dr. Peppers, and bakes tons of sweets.

Five things Ann's bio doesn't mention:

1. She's been married to the same man since dirt.

2. She loves to shop at thrift stores.

3. She hates talking on the phone.

4. A really sharp pencil makes her happy.

5. She's thankful wrinkles aren't painful.


You can contact Ann at ann.everett@rocketmail.com

You can visit her site at www.anneverett.com

Stalk her at:

http://www.twitter.com/TalkinTwang

http://www.linkedin.com/pub/ann-everett/38/482/968

http://www.Plus.google.com/108564049431137119227

http://www.pinterest.com/loacl/

http://on.fb.me/H0jCvv

# TABLE OF CONTENTS

INTRODUCTION..................................................6

ENTER/ENTERED...............................................9

FELT/SEEMED/SHOWED...................................13

GIVE/GAVE.......................................................18

HAVE/HAS/HAD................................................21

HEARD............................................................25

HELD...............................................................27

HIT..................................................................32

JUMP...............................................................36

KNOW/KNEW...................................................39

LEFT/EXITED...................................................41

LIE/LAY...........................................................44

LIKE/LIKED.....................................................46

LOOKED/SAW.................................................47

PUSH/PUSHED................................................51

PUT.................................................................54

RAN.................................................................58

REACTION WORDS..........................................60

SAID/ASKED……………………………………..65

SMELLED……………………………………...75

STOOD……………………………………76

TASTED/DRANK…………………………………...77

THOUGHT/REMEMBERED……………………….79

TOOK……………………………………………...82

TOUCH/TOUCHED………………………………..88

TURNED……………………………………………...91

WALK/WALKED……………………………………94

WAS/WERE……………………………………..99

# INTRODUCTION

## Verb,n.Grammar.

The key word in most sentences that reveals what is happening. It can declare something...*She looked*, or ask a question...*Did she look?*

Good definition, but why say *She looked*, if she can gawk, spy, or examine? The familiar choice offers vague action, where the stronger selection gives action and expression. Let's consider other examples.

In place of...*He felt*, use caressed, groped, fumbled.

Why write *Mary took* when fetched, scooped, or heaved are better descriptions?

The *detective pushed* doesn't show as much as the detective rammed, elbowed, or propelled.

If we didn't have verbs, where would a story go? *Nowhere*. Characters, animals, and nature can't *be* or *do* anything without a verb. Characters can't laugh, animals can't attack, and trees can't sway in the breeze. Verbs provide excitement, drive the narrative and paint a vivid picture in the readers' mind.

Verbs also determine when something happens, in the present, in the past, or in the future. They set the tense of your tale. Here are some examples:

Present tense—I/you/we/they drink --he/she/it drinks

Past tense—I/you/he/she/it/we/they drank

Future tense—I/you/he/she/it/we/they will drink

Present perfect tense—I/you/he/she/it/we/they have drunk

Past perfect tense—I/you/he/she/it/we/they had drunk

Future perfect tense—I/you/he/she/it/we/they will have drunk

  Using *Strong Verbs, Strong Voice*, authors can quickly replace dull, and over used verbs, giving their stories more punch and verve. Remember, you can add an s/es/ing/ed OR remove "ed" depending on the tense you're using.

In rough/first drafts, I use common verbs. Once I'm done with my manuscript, I take chapter by chapter, and do a word search replacing them with stronger choices.

## ONE LAST THING

For years, I gave part of this list as a hand-out when I spoke to writers' groups. I've received many emails stating how the substitutions proved helpful to recipients. This book is meant as a starting point for using more colorful and active verbs. I hope STRONG VERBS; STRONG VOICE will become one of your favorite resources.

# ENTER/ENTERED

Access

Alight

Appear/Appeared

Arrive

Barge in

Blow in

Bob up

Breeze in

Broke in

Burst in

Bust in

Butt in

Buzz in

Came in

Catalog

Chart

Check in

Clock in

Come/Came in

Compile

Compose

Crack

Crawl

Creep

Cross the threshold

Crowd in

Debarked

Descend

Dismount

Documented

Drive in

Drop anchor

Drop in

Enroll

## ENTER/ENTERED

| | |
|---|---|
| Enlist | Input |
| Enumerate | Insert |
| Fall by | Insinuate |
| Fall in | Intervene |
| Fall into | Introduce |
| Forced her/his way in | Intrude |
| Gain entry | Invade |
| Get to | Jot down |
| Get/Go/Got in | Jump in |
| Gust in | Key in |
| Hit town | Land/Landed |
| Horn in | List |
| Immigrated | Log |
| Infiltrated | Make it |
| Imported | Make the scene |
| Initiated | Make way |
| | Map |

**ENTER/ENTERED**

| | |
|---|---|
| Move in/into | Report |
| Note | Roll in |
| Pass into | Rush in |
| Penetrate | Sailed in |
| Perch | Set foot in/on |
| Perforate | Show up |
| Pierce | Sign in/up |
| Pile in | Slip in |
| Pop in | Sneak |
| Pull/Pulled in | Spring |
| Punch the clock | Stepped inside |
| Puncture | Submit |
| Put down | Take place |
| Reach/Reached | Tap in |
| Reached destination | Turn up |
| Record | Type in |
| Register | Visit |

**ENTER/ENTERED**

Volunteer for

Went in

Wind up at

Work in

Worm in

Wriggle

Write

# FELT/SEEMED/SHOWED

Accompany

Alluded to

Appeared/Appeared as

Assumed

Bared

Bear/Bear out

Believed

Bespoke

Betokened

Betrayed

Boiled

Caressed

Clasp

Clutch

Communicated

Compared

Comprehended

Conduct

Confirm

Connoted

Considered

Convey

Correlated

Corroborate

Deemed

Demonstrated

Depicted

Detected

Direct

Discerned

## FELT/SEEMED/SHOWED

| | |
|---|---|
| Disclosed | Frisked |
| Displayed | Fumbled |
| Emblematic of | Grapple |
| Entangle | Grasp |
| Escort | Grip |
| Establish | Grope |
| Evidenced | Guess |
| Exhibit/Exhibited | Guide |
| Experienced | Had every appearance of |
| Explore | Had the earmarks of |
| Exposed | Had the look of |
| Express | Handled |
| Figured | Hinted at |
| Fingered | Illustrate |
| Fondled | Implied |
| Foretokened | Indicated |
| Forewarned | Insinuate |

## FELT/SEEMED/SHOWED

| | |
|---|---|
| Instill | Manipulated |
| Instruct | Marked |
| Intimated | Maul |
| Intuit | Model |
| Investigated | Noticed |
| Judged | Obvious |
| Knew | Palm |
| Known | Pawed |
| Lay open | Perceive |
| Lead | Pinch |
| Lectured | Pin pointed |
| Looked as if | Pioneer |
| Looked like | Ply |
| Made manifest | Poke |
| Make plain | Portended |
| Mandated | Presaged |
| Manifested | Present |

## FELT/SEEMED/SHOWED

| | |
|---|---|
| Press | Struck her/him as |
| Pretend | Substantiate |
| Probed | Suffered |
| Proved | Suggested |
| Realigned | Suspected |
| Reckoned | Tangle |
| Resembled | Teach |
| Responded | Test |
| Revealed | Thought |
| Scrabbled | Tickle |
| Sensation | Touched |
| Sensed | Try |
| Signified | Twiddle |
| Snarl | Twine |
| Sounded like | Twist |
| Squeeze | Undergo/Undergone |
| Stroked | Understood |

## FELT/SEEMED/SHOWED

Underwent

Usher

Verify

Weave

Wield

# GIVE/GAVE

Abetted

Accommodated

Accorded

Afford

Aided

Allocated

Allotted

Assigned

Assisted

Awarded

Backed

Bequeathed

Bestowed

Break/Broke

Caused

Collapsed

Commissioned

Committed

Communicate

Conferred

Contributed

Convey

Cooperated

Cracked

Created

Crumbled

Dedicated

Delivered

Devoted

Did

Diffused

Disbursed

Discarded

Dispensed

## GIVE/GAVE

| | |
|---|---|
| Disposed | Issued |
| Ditched | Lend/Lent |
| Divided | Leveraged |
| Do | Offered |
| Donated | Organized |
| Enabled | Passed |
| Ended | Performed |
| Expedited | Presented |
| Facilitated | Produced |
| Fractured | Provided |
| Furnished | Reinforced |
| Generated | Relented |
| Go | Sacrificed |
| Granted | Separated |
| Handed | Served |
| Helped | Share |
| Imparted | Shattered |

**GIVE/GAVE**

| | |
|---|---|
| Smoothed | Submitted |
| Snapped | Supported |
| Spent | Surrendered |
| Split | Transferred |
| Sponsored | Undertook |
| Staged | Went |
| | Yielded |

# HAVE/HAS/HAD

| | |
|---|---|
| Accept | Bore |
| Acquire | Broaden |
| Adhere | Carried |
| Admit | Chalk up |
| Allocate | Claimed |
| Allow | Clasp |
| Anticipate | Clutched |
| Arrange | Collect |
| Assert | Compose |
| Ate | Comprise |
| Be affected by | Configure |
| Be ill with | Consume |
| Be inflicted with | Contain |
| Be necessary | Control |
| Be sick with | Covered |
| Betray | Cultivate |
| Boast | Dealt |

## HAVE/HAS/HAD

| | |
|---|---|
| Declare | Enjoy |
| Develop | Ensure |
| Diversify | Entertain |
| Devise | Erased |
| Devour | Evidenced |
| Display | Evinced |
| Distribute | Exhibited |
| Draft | Expanded |
| Drank/Drunk | Experienced |
| Earn | Extended |
| Eaten | Featured |
| Embrace | Formed |
| Empower | Gain/Gained |
| Enclose | Gather |
| Encompass | Gave |
| Endure | Generated |
| Enhance | Get hands on |

## HAVE/HAS/HAD

| | |
|---|---|
| Get hold of | Latch on to |
| Given | Maintained |
| Got/Gotten | Manufacture |
| Grant | Mobilized |
| Grapple | Must |
| Grasp | Needed |
| Grip | Nursed |
| Held | Obligated |
| Honed | Obtained |
| Hosts | Organized |
| Hustle | Originate |
| Included | Ought to |
| Incorporated | Owned |
| Initiated | Partaken |
| Invents | Partook |
| Involved | Permitted |
| Improved | Possessed |

**HAVE/HAS/HAD**

Produced

Received

Recoup

Required

Retained

Secured

Snagged

Spanned

Sported

Spread

Stated

Suffer from

Suffer with

Suffered

Suspended

Sustain

Take in

Taken

Tolerated

Took

Toted

Undergone

Underwent

Wielded

Wore

# HEARD

Absorbed

Adjudicate on

Appreciated

Apprehended

Attended to

Be informed

Be made aware

Be told

Caught

Cognized

Comprehended

Considered

Detected

Discovered

Earwigged

Eavesdropped

Examined

Fathomed

Find out

Gathered

Gave an ear to

Gave audience to

Get wind of

Gleaned

Got/gotten

Grasped

Harked

Heard him out

Hearkened

Heeded

Identified

Judge

Judged

Learned

Lent an ear to

Listened

| | |
|---|---|
| Listened in | Received |
| Meddled | Snooped |
| Memorized | Strained her ears |
| Out of earshot | Took heed of |
| Overheard | Took in |
| Perceived | Tried |
| Picked up | Understood |
| Realized | Within earshot |

# HELD

Abducted

Accepted

Accommodated

Achieved

Acquired

Adhered

Administered

Affirmed

Aligned

Alleged

Apprehended

Arbitrate

Arranged

Arrested

Assembled

Assumed

Attached

Balanced

Barred

Believed

Bore

Bound

Called

Carried

Carry on

Chaired

Championed

Claimed

Clasped

Clutched

Commanded

Comprised

Concluded

Conducted

**HELD**

| | |
|---|---|
| Confined | Dominated |
| Connected | Draw out |
| Conserved | Embraced |
| Considered | Employed |
| Contained | Enfolded |
| Continued | Engaged |
| Controlled | Enjoyed |
| Convened | Enlisted |
| Coordinated | Enveloped |
| Credited | Execute |
| Cuddled | Exhibited |
| Declared | Experienced |
| Deemed | Extended |
| Defended | Fastened |
| Detained | Felt |
| Determined | Financed |
| Displayed | Fixed |

**HELD**

| | |
|---|---|
| Fortified | Judged |
| Funded | Kept |
| Gathered | Labeled |
| Gauged | Lasted |
| Govern | Linked |
| Grasped | Lock up |
| Gripped | Maintained |
| Guarded | Managed |
| Had | Moderated |
| Hang on | Monopolized |
| Hem in | Occupied |
| Hired | Opined |
| Hold on | Orchestrate |
| Hugged | Organized |
| Imprisoned | Oversee |
| Incarcerated | Owned |
| Joined | Partnered |

## HELD

| | |
|---|---|
| Persisted | Scheduled |
| Pin down | Seated |
| Possessed | Secured |
| Prepared | Seized |
| Preserve | Shouldered |
| Presumed | Showed |
| Professed | Spanned |
| Run/Ran | Sported |
| Reckoned | Squeezed |
| Recruited | Stood |
| Regarded | Stored |
| Remanded | Stowed |
| Reserve | Stretch out |
| Resisted | Stuck |
| Restrained | Supported |
| Retained | Supposed |
| Said | Surmised |

**HELD**

| | |
|---|---|
| Suspended | Undertook |
| Sustained | United |
| Taken | Viewed |
| Thought | Waited |
| Toted | Wedged |
| Trusted | Whispered |
| Tucked | Wielded |
| Understood | Wore/Worn |

# HIT

Abused

Affect

Annihilated

Assail

Attacked

Banged

Bashed

Battered

Bear upon

Beat/Beaten

Belted

Blow

Boxed

Branded

Bumped

Chopped

Clapped

Clipped

Clobbered

Clocked

Clout

Clubbed

Collided

Conquered

Cracked

Crashed

Creamed

Crushed

Cuffed

Cut

## HIT

Damaged

Decked

Defeated

Demolished

Destroyed

Devastate

Donged

Double-decked

Doused

Drubbed

Ended

Eradicated

Extinguished

Flayed

Flogged

Ground

Hacked

Hammered

Hurtled

Iced

Impacted

Injure

Jarred

Karate Chopped

Knock sideways

Knocked

Lashed

Licked

Macerated

Maim

Milled

Minced

Molested

Obliterated

**HIT**

| | |
|---|---|
| Peg | Shattered |
| Perforated | Slam dunked |
| Pin | Slammed |
| Ploughed | Slapped |
| Pommeled | Slashed |
| Pounded | Slugged |
| Pulped | Smacked |
| Pulverized | Smashed |
| Pummeled | Smitten |
| Pumped | Smote |
| Punched | Socked |
| Rammed | Spanked |
| Rang his bell | Spike |
| Rapped | Stamped |
| Ripped | Stricken |
| Ruined | Strike/Struck |
| Run/Ran into | Swiped |

**HIT**

| | |
|---|---|
| Swung | Touch on |
| Tackled | Traumatize |
| Tap | Trounced |
| Tapped | Upset |
| Tattooed | Violated |
| Terminated | Walloped |
| Thrashed | Whacked |
| Throttled | Whipped |
| Thumped | Wound |
| Thwacked | Wrecked |

# JUMP

| | |
|---|---|
| Ambushed | Dived |
| Assault | Dove |
| Attack | Ejected |
| Bobbed | Erupted |
| Bobbled | Exploded |
| Bounced | Fired |
| Bounded | Flinched |
| Buck | Flung |
| Cavort | Fly/Flew |
| Charged | Frolic |
| Cleared | Hike |
| Climb | Hopped |
| Cringed | Hurled |
| Dance | Hurtled |
| Dashed | Jerked |

**JUMP**

| | |
|---|---|
| Jig | Rebounded |
| Jolted | Recoil |
| Jut/Jutted | Reeled |
| Launched | Rise |
| Leapt/Leaped | Rocketed |
| Lunged | Sail over |
| Lurched | Seize upon |
| Mount | Shot up/shot from |
| Move | Shudder |
| Parachuted | Skipped |
| Pitched | Skyrocket |
| Plunged | Snatched |
| Pogoed | Soar |
| Pounced | Spasm |
| Prance | Sprang/Sprung |
| Propelled | Started |
| Quaked | Startled |

**JUMP**

Surge

Swooped

Thrust

Tumbled

Upsurge

Upswing

Vaulted

Wax

Wheeled

# KNOW/KNEW

| | |
|---|---|
| Accept | Fathom |
| Acquainted | Find out |
| Appreciate | Follow |
| Assimilate | Found |
| Behold | Got |
| Catch on | Grasp |
| Comprehend | Hear |
| Conceive | Identified |
| Decipher | Imagine |
| Decode | Intuit |
| Differentiate | Learn |
| Dig | Lived through |
| Discern | Notice |
| Discovered | Mastered |
| Distinguished | Penetrate |
| Endure | Perceive |
| Experience | Pick up |
| Familiarize | Pierce |

## KNOW/KNEW

Possess

Prize

Realized

Recognize

Register

Savvy

Saw

Seize

Sensed

Suffer

Sustain

Take in

Told

Track

Undergo

Understand

Underwent

Visualized

Witness

# LEFT/EXITED

| | |
|---|---|
| Abandon | Departed |
| Absconded | Deserted |
| Advanced | Disappeared |
| Allowed | Ditched |
| Avoided | Donated |
| Beat a hasty retreat | Dropped |
| Beat it | Dump |
| Bequeathed | Effected |
| Bolted | Ensued |
| Bowed out | Escaped |
| Check out | Exhausted |
| Cleared out | Entrusted |
| Consigned | Exodus |
| Continued | Expended |
| Caused | Faded |
| Decamped | Flee/Fled |
| Deferred | Flight |
| Delayed | Forsook/Forsaken |

## LEFT/EXITED

| | |
|---|---|
| Get away/Get out | Permitted |
| Get going | Place |
| Go forth | Proceeded |
| Gone | Progressed |
| Hand over | Push off |
| Head off | Quit |
| Head out | Ran off |
| Hightailed | Renounced |
| Jilted | Resign |
| Leave | Retired |
| Leave behind | Retreated |
| Leave high and dry | Run for it |
| Legated | Sallied forth |
| Make a break for it | Scarpered |
| Make a move | Set forth/off |
| Make a run for it | Set sail |
| Make tracks | Shove off |
| Move | Skirted |

**LEFT/EXITED**

| | |
|---|---|
| Split | Vacate |
| Step down | Vamoosed |
| Take leave | Vanished |
| Take off | Walked away |
| Took off | Walked off |
| | Went out |
| | Withdrew |

# LIE/LAY

Do you get confused about when to use lie or lay? You're not alone! I like to simplify by saying if it's a person reclining, it's always *lie,* but if you're placing something, it's *lay.* Most of the time that simplification will work… but it really has to do with having an object or not. For instance, in my definition, you'd think *Now I lay me down to sleep* is wrong and should be *Now I lie me down to sleep* because "I" is reclining…BUT in this example "ME" is the object, so lay is correct.

Remember in order to use lie and lay correctly, lie is a "to be" verb without an object and means to recline or rest. Lay means to place, put, or set something down (an object) like a book, cup, or eye glasses, etc.

You can solve the dilemma by choosing a stronger verb!

Of course in dialogue, your characters can use lie and lay incorrectly unless they are supposed to be smart enough to know the rule!

| | |
|---|---|
| Be recumbent | Drooped |
| Collapsed | Dropped |
| Crashed | Dwell |
| Crumpled | Eased onto |
| Displaced | Fell |
| Dissolved | Fizzled |

## LIE/LAY

| | |
|---|---|
| Flopped onto | Recumbent |
| Folded | Relaxed |
| Idled | Remain |
| Keep | Reposed |
| Lazed | Rested |
| Leaned | Sagged |
| Lolled | Sank |
| Lounged | Set |
| Luxuriated | Shut down |
| Moved | Sit/Sat |
| Place | Situated |
| Placed | Slouched |
| Pose | Slumped |
| Positioned | Sprawled |
| Prone | Stop |
| Prostrate | Stretched out |
| Put/Put down | Supine |
| Reclined | Wilted |

# LIKE/LIKED

Admire

Adore/Adored

Aped

Appealed

Caricatured

Copycatted

Duplicated

Enjoy

Emulated

Fond of

Imitated

Keen on

Love

Mimicked

Mirrored

Mocked

Parodied

Partial to

Relish

Revel in

Represented

Take pleasure in

# LOOKED/SAW

Aimed
Analyze
Appraise
Ascertain
Assayed
Assess
Beam
Beheld
Calculated
Canvassed
Cast a glance
Catch sight of
Checked
Conceived
Consider
Contemplate
Detect

Diagnosed
Discerned
Dissected
Distinguish
Envisaged
Envisioned
Espied
Evaluate
Examine
Explored
Eyeballed
Eyed
Eyes begged
Fancied
Fixated
Fixed with a stare
Flipped through

## LOOKED/SAW

| | |
|---|---|
| Focused | Identified |
| Frowned | Imagined |
| Gaped | Inspect |
| Gawk | Investigate |
| Gawped | Judged |
| Gaze | Kept in sight |
| Get/Got a load of | Kept watch |
| Glance | Leer |
| Glanced off | Made out |
| Glanced through | Magnified |
| Glared | Met |
| Glimpse | Monitored |
| Glowered | Noted |
| Goggled | Noticed |
| Grimace | Observe |
| Grinned | Ogled |
| Held in view | Peek |

## LOOKED/SAW

- Peep
- Peered
- Perceived
- Perused
- Pictured
- Reassess
- Recognize
- Reconnoiter
- Reconsider
- Reexamine
- Regard
- Remark
- Research
- Revaluated
- Rubbernecked
- Scan
- Scoured
- Scowl
- Scrutinize
- Search
- Sense
- Shot him a look
- Sighted
- Sized up
- Skimmed
- Smirk
- Sneered
- Snooped
- Spied
- Spotted
- Squinted
- Stared
- Stood guard
- Studied

**LOOKED/SAW**

Surveyed

Take a gander

Took in

Took stock of

Viewed

Visualized

Watched

Witnessed

# PUSH/PUSHED

| | |
|---|---|
| Activate | Duel |
| Advanced | Elbowed |
| Advocated | Encouraged |
| Backed | Endorsed |
| Ballasted | Exhort |
| Blasted | Fight |
| Bolster | Flung |
| Boosted | Forced |
| Bundle | Forged ahead |
| Cast | Forwarded |
| Clash | Goad |
| Coerce | Heaved |
| Deal | Hustled |
| Displace | Impelled |
| Drove/Driven | Inched |

## PUSH/PUSHED

| | |
|---|---|
| Incited | Persuade |
| Increased | Press |
| Induce | Pressed forward |
| Inspired | Prodded |
| Jammed | Promote |
| Jolted | Prompted |
| Jostled | Propelled |
| Labor | Provoke |
| Lobbed | Rammed |
| Made way | Roused |
| Make | Send |
| Motivated | Set in motion |
| Nagged | Shouldered |
| Nudged | Shoved |
| Operate | Shunted |
| Plugged | Spurred |
| Poked | Squeezed through |

**PUSH/PUSHED**

| | |
|---|---|
| Struggle | Trundled |
| Sweep | Twisted |
| Threw | Urged |
| Thrown | Wedged |
| Thrust | Worked |
| Trade | Wrestled |
| Travel | |

# PUT

| | |
|---|---|
| Accommodate | Customize |
| Adapt | Dedicated |
| Add | Deposit |
| Alter | Devoted |
| Apply | Displayed |
| Appoint | Donated |
| Approximate | Drape |
| Arrange | Drop |
| Articulate | Dump |
| Assign | Dunk |
| Cast | Eased |
| Cater | Employ |
| Change | Equipped |
| Consign | Estimate |
| Convert | Evaluate |
| Crammed | Exert |

## PUT

| | |
|---|---|
| Expend | Lay/Laid |
| Fling/Flung | Leave |
| Formulate | Loaded |
| Frame | Lobbed |
| Furnished | Lodged |
| Gauge | Modify |
| Grade | Mounted |
| Guess | Organize |
| Heave | Orientate |
| Hurl | Parked |
| Implement | Perch |
| Individualize | Phrase |
| Insert | Pinned |
| Install | Place |
| Interposed | Plant |
| Invest | Pledged |
| Judge | Plonk |

**PUT**

| | |
|---|---|
| Plopped | Set before |
| Plunked | Set upright |
| Plunked down | Shifted |
| Pop | Situate |
| Posed | Slapped on |
| Posited | Sort |
| Position | Spend |
| Prepare | Stash |
| Propose | Stationed |
| Provided | Stick |
| Rank | Stood on end |
| Rate | Strapped |
| Recommend | Stuck |
| Redact | Stuffed |
| Relegate | Subject |
| Set | Supplied |
| Settle | Switch |

**PUT**

Threw                    Utilized

Tossed

Upended

# RAN

Accelerated

Barreled

Bustled

Charged

Competed

Continued

Coursed

Darted

Dashed

Entered

Expedite

Filed

Flashed

Flew

Flooded

Flowed

Gushed

Hiked

Hobbled

Hopped

Hurled

Hurried

Hurtled

Jogged

Loped

Lurched

Marched

Paced

Persisted

Poured out

Proceeded

Pursued

Quick stepped

Reached

**RAN**

| | |
|---|---|
| Rushed | Sped |
| Scampered | Spilled |
| Scooted | Sprinted |
| Scrambled | Streamed |
| Scuffed | Stumbled |
| Scurried | Tracked |
| Scuttled | Trickled |
| Shot | Tripped |
| Shuffled | Trotted |
| | Zoom |

# REACTION WORDS

Anger rose along with voice

Admitted

Balked

Beamed

Bit lip

Blanched

Blinked

Blushed

Cackled

Cheeks reddened

Chortled

Chuckled

Color bloomed

Color rose in cheeks

Cocked head

Cringed

Dillydallied

Drooped

Exhaled

Eyes narrowed

Eyes widened

Face pinched

Face reddened

Faltered

Fell silent

Flashed a grin

Flicked

Flinched

Flung

Flushed

Frowned

Fumed

## REACTION WORDS

| | |
|---|---|
| Gasped | Laughed |
| Giggled | Leered |
| Glanced | Listed |
| Glared | Moaned |
| Grimaced | Mocked |
| Grinned | Moped |
| Groaned | Nodded |
| Gulped | Panted |
| Guzzled | Paused |
| Heave a sigh | Peeked |
| Hesitated | Pooh-poohed |
| High-fived | Pouted |
| Huffed | Puffed |
| Interchanged | Quivered |
| Inhaled | Raged |
| Keeled over | Raised brow |

# REACTION

- Ranted
- Reclined
- Recoiled
- Reeled
- Rejoiced
- Relaxed
- Released breath
- Relished
- Resisted
- Retracted
- Retreated
- Rocked
- Scanned
- Scoffed
- Scowled
- Seethed
- Shifted
- Shillyshallied
- Shivered
- Shook
- Shrieked
- Shook
- Shook head
- Shouted
- Shrugged
- Shuddered
- Sighed
- Simpered
- Skimmed
- Slackened
- Smiled
- Smirked
- Sneered
- Snickered

# REACTION

| | |
|---|---|
| Sniffed | Swayed |
| Snorted | Swigged |
| Squinted | Thawed |
| Staggered | Tilted |
| Stared | Tilted head |
| Started | Toasted |
| Startled | Took deep breath |
| Stiffened | Trembled |
| Stifled yawn/laugh | Twirled around |
| Strained | Twirled hair around finger |
| Stretched | Twisted hair |
| Stumbled | Twisted head |
| Sucked in a breath | Twisted in seat/chair |
| Sulked | Twitched |
| Swallowed | Wheezed |

**REACTION**

Wiggled          Wobbled

Winced           Yawned

Winked           Yielded

# SAID/ASKED

Don't misunderstand. There is nothing wrong with using *said or asked* in your tag/attribution. As a matter of fact, many think it's better to use those instead of other synonyms. But, sometimes a different word choice conveys more. If your character is southern, you may want her to drawl. If they're drunk, they may need to slur or lisp.

| | |
|---|---|
| Accused | Argued |
| Acknowledged | Articulated |
| Added | Ascribed |
| Addressed | Asserted |
| Admitted | Assumed |
| Advanced | Assured |
| Advised | Authorized |
| Affirmed | Averred |
| Agreed | Avouched |
| Aired | Avowed |
| Announced | Babbled |
| Answered | Bantered |
| Approved | Barked |

## SAID/ASKED

| | |
|---|---|
| Bawled | Bubbled |
| Beamed | Bugged |
| Begged | Cackled |
| Belittled | Called |
| Bellowed | Came out with |
| Berated | Cautioned |
| Beseeched | Chastised |
| Betrayed | Challenged |
| Blasted | Chatted |
| Blathered | Chattered |
| Bleated | Cheered |
| Blurted | Chided |
| Boasted | Chimed |
| Boomed | Chirped |
| Bragged | Choked |
| Breathed | Chortled |
| Broadcast | Chorused |
| Broke in | Chuckled |

## SAID/ASKED

| | |
|---|---|
| Cited | Convinced |
| Claimed | Cooed |
| Clarified | Copied |
| Clashed | Corrected |
| Clucked | Corresponded |
| Coaxed | Coughed |
| Commanded | Counseled |
| Commented | Cried |
| Complained | Cried out |
| Completed | Croaked |
| Conceded | Crooned |
| Concluded | Crowed |
| Confessed | Dared |
| Confided | Decided |
| Congratulated | Declaimed |
| Consoled | Declared |
| Continued | Decreed |
| Conveyed | Dedicated |

## SAID/ASKED

- Defined
- Delegated
- Demanded
- Denied
- Described
- Digressed
- Disagreed
- Disclosed
- Disparaged
- Dictated
- Divulged
- Drawled
- Drilled
- Droned
- Edited
- Echoed
- Elaborated
- Enlightened
- Enunciated
- Exclaimed
- Explained
- Expressed
- Faltered
- Finished
- Flapped
- Flattered
- Flirted
- Fretted
- Gabbled
- Gasped
- Gibbered
- Giggled
- Gossiped
- Grated
- Greeted
- Grilled
- Griped

## SAID/ASKED

| | |
|---|---|
| Groaned | Hypothesized |
| Growled | Imagined |
| Grumbled | Imitated |
| Grunted | Imparted |
| Guaranteed | Implied |
| Guessed | Implored |
| Guffawed | Imputed |
| Gulped | Indicted |
| Gurgled | Induce |
| Gushed | Informed |
| Hailed | Inquired |
| Harangued | Interceded |
| Harassed | Interjected |
| Hiccupped | Interviewed |
| Hinted | Intoned |
| Hissed | Insinuated |
| Hollered | Insisted |
| Howled | Instructed |

**SAID/ASKED**

| | |
|---|---|
| Interrupted | Mentored |
| Jabbed | Mimicked |
| Jabbered | Moaned |
| Jeered | Mocked |
| Jested | Mumbled |
| Joked | Murmured |
| Lamented | Mused |
| Laughed | Muttered |
| Let Slip | Nagged |
| Let out | Named |
| Lied | Narrated |
| Lisped | Nattered |
| Lobbied | Nodded |
| Made known | Nominated |
| Maintained | Noted |
| Marveled | Notified |
| Maundered | Objected |
| Mentioned | Observed |

**SAID/ASKED**

| | |
|---|---|
| Offered | Proclaimed |
| Ordered | Professed |
| Outwitted | Promised |
| Panted | Prompted |
| Parroted | Pronounced |
| Petitioned | Proposed |
| Piped | Protested |
| Pleaded | Purported |
| Pledged | Put before |
| Pointed out | Put in |
| Pondered | Puzzled |
| Pontificated | Quavered |
| Praised | Queried |
| Prated | Questioned |
| Prattled | Quipped |
| Prayed | Quoted |
| Preached | Raged |
| Predicted | Rambled |

## SAID/ASKED

| | |
|---|---|
| Ranted | Retorted |
| Rattled | Revealed |
| Raved | Rhapsodized |
| Recorded | Roared |
| Reasoned | Sang out |
| Reassured | Sassed |
| Recalled | Scoffed |
| Recited | Scolded |
| Reckoned | Screamed |
| Related | Screeched |
| Remarked | Sermonized |
| Remembered | Shouted |
| Reminded | Shrieked |
| Repeated | Shrilled |
| Replied | Sighed |
| Reported | Slurred |
| Requested | Smiled |
| Responded | Smirked |

## SAID/ASKED

| | |
|---|---|
| Snapped | Stammered |
| Snarled | Strangled |
| Sneered | Started |
| Sneezed | Stated |
| Snickered | Steamed |
| Sniffed | Stormed |
| Sniffled | Stuttered |
| Snorted | Suggested |
| Sobbed | Summoned |
| Solicited | Surmised |
| Spat | Swore |
| Speculated | Tattled |
| Spoke | Taunted |
| Spouted | Teased |
| Sputtered | Tempted |
| Squawked | Tested |
| Squeaked | Theorized |
| Squealed | Threatened |

## SAID/ASKED

| | |
|---|---|
| Thundered | Wept |
| Told | Whimpered |
| Twittered | Whined |
| Urged | Whispered |
| Uttered | Wigwagged |
| Vaunted | Wisecracked |
| Vented | Wondered aloud |
| Voiced | Worried |
| Volunteered | Yakked |
| Vowed | Yawned |
| Wailed | Yelled |
| Warned | Yelped |

# Smelled

| | |
|---|---|
| Assaulted the nostrils | Reeked |
| Breathed in | Savored |
| Detected | Scented |
| Discerned | Sensed |
| Evoke | Sniffed |
| Filled lungs | Sniveled |
| Get a whiff | Snorted |
| Huffed | Snuffed |
| Inhaled | Snuffled |
| Niffed | Suck in |
| Perceived | Suspected |
| Ponged | Take in |
| Puffed | Tasted |
| Pull in | Whiffed |

# STOOD

| | |
|---|---|
| Erected | Remained upright |
| Elevated | Righted himself/herself |
| Got to his feet | Rose |
| Heaved | Rose to his feet |
| Held herself erect | Stationed herself |
| Hoisted | Straightened |
| Jumped up | Uplifted |
| Lifted | Upraised |
| Mounted | Winched |
| Raised | |
| Reared | |

# TASTED/DRANK

| | |
|---|---|
| Bit into | Imbibed |
| Chewed | Ingested |
| Chomped | Knock back |
| Chugged | Lapped |
| Consume | Licked |
| Crunched | Masticated |
| Discerned | Melted |
| Distinguished | Munched |
| Downed | Nipped |
| Drained | Quaffed |
| Experience | Quenched |
| Experimented | Relished |
| Glugged | Ruminated |
| Gnawed | Sampled |
| Ground | Sank teeth into |
| Gulped | Savored |
| Guzzled | Sipped |

## TASTED/DRANK

| | |
|---|---|
| Slammed back | Swallowed |
| Slurped | Swigged |
| Smacked | Swilled |
| Soused | Swilled down |
| Sucked | Tested |
| Suckled | Tippled |
| Supped | Tried |
| | Washed down |

# THOUGHT/REMEMBER

Accepted

Acknowledged

Admitted

Aimed

Allowed

Anticipated

Assessed

Associate

Brooded

Brought to mind

Called to mind

Came to her

Cite

Commemorate

Conceived

Concentrated

Concluded

Concocted

Confessed

Conjured

Connect

Considered

Contemplated

Critiqued

Decided

Deduced

Deliberated

Designed

Dreamed

Enabled

Entertained the notion/idea

Envisaged

Envisioned

Esteemed

Expected

Extrapolated

## THOUGHT/REMEMBERED

| | |
|---|---|
| Fabricated | Judged |
| Fancied | Kept in mind |
| Fashioned | Knew |
| Feared | Link |
| Featured | Memorize |
| Finalized | Mention |
| Flirted with | Meditated |
| Formed | Mulled |
| Formulated | Mused |
| Gauged | Name |
| Guessed | Noticed |
| Hatched | Occurred to her |
| Held in mind | Pictured |
| Hoped | Planned |
| Imagined | Pondered |
| Inferred | Pretended |
| Intended | Projected |
| | Realized |

## THOUGHT/REMEMBERED

- Reasoned
- Recalled
- Recognized
- Recollected
- Reconsidered
- Refer
- Reflected
- Relate
- Reminisce
- Retain
- Retrieve
- Reviewed
- Ruminated
- Simulated
- Studied
- Supposed
- Suspected
- Through better of it
- Turned it over in her/his mind
- Understood
- Weighed
- Went over
- Willed
- Wondered

# TOOK

Abided
Abolish
Accepted
Accommodated
Accumulated
Acknowledged
Acquired
Adopted
Amassed
Annexed
Appreciated
Appropriated
Assumed
Ate
Balanced
Benefitted
Bought
Brought

Captured
Carried
Carted
Caught
Chose
Claimed
Cleared
Collar
Collected
Commandeered
Commenced
Compiled
Conducted
Controlled
Conquered
Considered
Consumed
Contained

**TOOK**

| | |
|---|---|
| Conveyed | Elected |
| Created | Elevated |
| Debated | Elicited |
| Deduced | Eliminated |
| Deducted | Embezzled |
| Deemed | Engineered |
| Delivered | Ensnared |
| Delved | Escorted |
| Demanded | Evicted |
| Derived | Examined |
| Designated | Expel |
| Discarded | Expended |
| Discussed | Experienced |
| Disposed | Extracted |
| Dominated | Extricated |
| Downed | Fetched |
| Dragged | Fielded |
| Drew | Fingered |

# TOOK

| | |
|---|---|
| Forced | Improvised |
| Gained | Interpreted |
| Garnered | Jimmied |
| Gathered | Juggled |
| Generated | Kidnapped |
| Gleaned | Led |
| Got | Lifted |
| Govern | Liquidated |
| Grabbed | Looted |
| Grasped | Lowered |
| Gripped | Lugged |
| Guided | Managed |
| Gulped | Molded |
| Hauled | Mustered |
| Heaved | Nabbed |
| Held | Needed |
| Hoisted | Negotiate |
| Hijacked | Nicked |

## TOOK

| | |
|---|---|
| Nurture | Prioritize |
| Occupied | Processed |
| Obtained | Procured |
| Outdistanced | Produced |
| Overcame | Pulled |
| Packed | Purchased |
| Picked | Raided |
| Pilfered | Raised |
| Pillaged | Ransacked |
| Pinched | Ravaged |
| Pirated | Read |
| Plucked | Received |
| Plundered | Regarded |
| Poached | Removed |
| Pocketed | Rented |
| Pondered | Required |
| Presumed | Rescued |
| Pried open | Restrict |

## TOOK

| | |
|---|---|
| Retrieved | Stripped |
| Rifled | Succeeded |
| Robbed | Sucked |
| Rooted out | Suffered |
| Sacked | Swallowed |
| Salvaged | Swapped |
| Scooped | Swept |
| Secured | Swigged |
| Seized | Swilled |
| Selected | Swiped |
| Shipped | Tasted |
| Showed | Taught |
| Sipped | Thieved |
| Snared | Tolerated |
| Snatched | Towed |
| Snatched out/up | Transferred |
| Snitched | Transmit |
| Stole | Transported |

**TOOK**

Trapped

Tugged

Understood

Undertook

Used

Ushered

Waited

Withdrew

Won

Worked

Wrangled

Wrought

Wrenched

Wrested

Yanked

# TOUCH/TOUCHED

| | |
|---|---|
| Advert | Flicked |
| Alighted | Flipped |
| Allude | Flogged |
| Attained | Fondled |
| Bedaubed | Fumbled |
| Brushed | Glanced |
| Care | Goaded |
| Caressed | Gouged |
| Comprehend | Grazed |
| Concern | Groped |
| Contacted | Handle |
| Cuddled | Handled |
| Dabbed | Held |
| Dappled | Hint |
| Drummed | Hugged |
| Fiddled | Impress |
| Fingered | Influence |
| Flattened | Jabbed |

## TOUCH/TOUCHED

| | |
|---|---|
| Jimmied | Petted |
| Jingled | Pinched |
| Kneaded | Poked |
| Knifed | Preened |
| Lobby | Pressed |
| Manage | Pried |
| Maneuvered | Primped |
| Mangled | Prodded |
| Manipulated | Promote |
| Massaged | Propped |
| Mauled | Pulled |
| Meet | Pumped |
| Nuzzled | Pushed |
| Palmed | Rapped |
| Palpated | Rattled |
| Patted | Reached |
| Pawed | Relate |
| | Rubbed |

## TOUCH/TOUCHED

Rummaged through
Scooped up
Scoured
Scraped
Scratched
Scrubbed
Shoved
Smeared
Smoothed
Squeezed
Strike
Trapped
Tugged
Twiddled
Twisted

Stroked
Stubbed
Suggest
Swept across
Tamped
Tapped
Thumbed
Ticked
Toyed
Wedged
Wiggled
Worked
Wrung

# TURNED

| | |
|---|---|
| Adapt | Diverted |
| Aimed | Eddied |
| Alter | Explained |
| Angled off | Flipped |
| Adjusted | Flex |
| Bend/bent | Focused |
| Changed | Formed |
| Circled | Go round |
| Coiled | Grow |
| Concentrated | Gyrated |
| Converted | Innovated |
| Corkscrewed | Looped |
| Crisscrossed | Meander |
| Crooked | Meandered |
| Curved | Modernized |
| Deform | Modify |
| Directed | Navigated |
| Divagated | Orient |

## TURNED

| | |
|---|---|
| Perform | Shape |
| Piloted | Sheered |
| Pirouetted | Shifted |
| Pivoted | Snaked |
| Pointed | Spin/Spun |
| Reeled | Spun on her heels |
| Regulated | Swirled |
| Remodeled | Swiveled |
| Rendered | Targeted |
| Renewed | Transformed |
| Renovated | Translated |
| Reorganized | Trundled |
| Revealed | Twined |
| Reversed | Twirled |
| Revolutionized | Twisted |
| Revolved | Twisted to one side |
| Rolled | Uncover |
| Rotated | Updated |

## TURNED

Veered

Weaved

Wheeled around

Whirled about

Wind

Wound

Wove

Wrenched

Zigzagged

# WALK/WALKED

| | |
|---|---|
| Absconded | Crossed |
| Advanced | Danced |
| Ambled | Darted |
| Ambulated | Dashed |
| Approached | Decamped |
| Ascended | Descended |
| Backtracked | Dodged |
| Bolted | Dog paddled |
| Bushwhacked | Drifted |
| Cantered | Eased |
| Careened | Edged |
| Charged | Eloped |
| Chased | Eluded |
| Climbed | Emerged |
| Continued | Entered |
| Covered ground | Escaped |
| Crawled | Evacuated |
| Crept | Evaded |

## WALK/WALKED

| | |
|---|---|
| Exited | Jogged |
| Filed | Launched |
| Flaunted | Leaped |
| Fled | Limped |
| Flew | Listed |
| Flitted | Loped |
| Floated | Lumbered |
| Frolicked | Lunged |
| Galloped | Lurched |
| Glided | Marched |
| Groped his way | Meandered |
| Hastened | Minced |
| Hauled off | Moved |
| Hiked | Paced |
| Hobbled | Paraded |
| Hurried | Parry |
| Hurtled | Passed |
| Inched | Patrolled |

## WALK/WALKED

| | |
|---|---|
| Perambulated | Sauntered |
| Perused | Scaled |
| Piggy-backed | Scampered |
| Pitter-pattered | Scooted |
| Plodded | Scrambled |
| Plowed | Scudded |
| Pranced | Scuffed |
| Proceeded | Scurried |
| Propelled | Shadowed |
| Prowled | Shambled |
| Pursued | Shuffled |
| Pussyfooted | Sidestepped |
| Raced | Sidled |
| Roamed | Skidded |
| Rove | Skipped |
| Rushed | Sling/slung |
| Sailed | Slithered |
| Sashayed | Slouched |

## WALK/WALKED

Sneaked

Snuck

Sprinted

Staggered

Stalked

Stamped

Staggered

Steered

Stepped

Stole

Stomped

Strayed

Strode

Strolled

Strutted

Stumbled

Swaggered

Swerved

Swished

Tangoed

Tap-danced

Tiptoed

Took flight

Tore

Trailed after

Traipsed

Tramped

Trampled

Traversed

Treaded

Trekked

Trespassed

Tripped

Trod/trodden

Trucked

Trudged

## WALK/WALKED

Ushered

Veered

Waddled

Waded

Waltzed

Wandered

Wended

Withdrew

Wobbled

# WAS/WERE

Bechanced

Contained

Existed

Happened

Hovered

Hung

Loomed

Occupied

Occurred

Perched

Persisted

Prevailed

Remained

Spanned

Stayed

Stood

Took place

Took up

Transpired

# RECOMMENDED READING

*Character: The Heartbeat of the Novel* (James R. Callan)

*The Emotion Thesaurus* (Angela Ackerman & Becca Puglisi)

*The 38 Most Common Fiction Writing Mistakes* (Jack M. Bickham)

Dear Reader,

If you found STRONG VERBS~ STRONG VOICE a useful reference, I'd love to hear from you. Honest reviews on Amazon and Goodreads are always appreciated. And if you would like to explore my novels, full of *Southern Sass and Texas Twang*, please visit:

http://www.anneverett.com

Best Regards,

~Ann

# ANN EVERETT BOOKS

*Romantic Suspense/Mystery Trilogy*

Laid Out and Candle Lit—Book One

You're Busting My Nuptials—Book Two

Tied With a Bow and No Place to Go—Book Three

*New Adult Romance*

Tell Me a Secret

Made in the USA
Middletown, DE
15 June 2017